No Barriers, No Limits!

ANDREA FREEMAN

ISBN: 978-0-615-69605-8

Published in U.S. by Changing Lives And
Sincerely Supporting You

Contents

Acknowledgements

God: First giving honor to God, who is the head of my life. I am truly grateful for all that You have done for my family and I. Thank You for never giving up on me. Even when I haven't been very deserving, You never turned Your back on me. You said in Your word, that You would never leave nor forsake me. Your word has NEVER come back void. I love You and I magnify Your name!

Grandmom and Granddad: To my grandparents, William and Easter Hooks: I truly love and thank you both for laying the foundation and planting seeds of greatness in my life. I have often wondered, "Where would I be, if it hadn't been for you two?" Well, God knew His plan for my life, and it was not meant for me to be without you. You two have been my ROCK and will always have a special place, while holding the key to my heart FOREVER! I love and miss you two very much....R.I.P.

Mom: Mommy, thank you for being my reason and my desire to live life to the best of my ability. You had always encouraged me and challenged me to do better. It's through remembering your words and actions as a

5

parent, that I have the motivation and determination to BECOME A BETTER ME, each and every day. Words cannot express my gratitude for having you as a mother, and I will strive to continue to make positive changes in my life, just as you had always wished I would. YOU ARE MY HERO AND MY ROLE MODEL!...I love you from the bottom of my heart....R.I.P.

Dad: Dad, thank you for being one of the best dads ever. There is nothing that you have not provided for me. You have always supported me and kept the faith, trust, and belief that one day, I would be well accomplished. YOU HAVE NEVER LET ME DOWN!....I love you more than words can say!

Children: Shalise, Shanise, Alexus, and Ayana, thanks for being four of the best daughters that a mother could ever ask for. You are the ones who inspire me to keep pressing forward, to reach my maximum potential. In spite of all of the struggles of being a single mother; you have always appreciated how hard I worked to provide for you all, commended me, and given me the highest praise as a mother. YOU ARE MY STRENGTH! I love you all, with all of me!

Brother: J.D. Dyson, although you are my baby brother, you have played a major role in being like a "BIG BROTHER" in my life. You have been there through all of the storms, trials, and tribulations. When all else failed, I COULD ALWAYS CALL ON YOU! There is no amount of money in the world, or anything else that I could do or give, to ever repay you for all that you have done for my family and I. You exemplify nothing less than the BEST EVER!....I love and admire you, more than any man on earth!

Chenel Banks: Chenel, you are my dearest and best friend EVER! Thank you for all of your help and support during the many journeys of my life. Thank you for your support while I was writing this book. You will always be the FIRST PLACE friend in my heart. Thank you for being a TRUE DIAMOND!...I love you and YOU ARE IRREPLACEABLE!

Author Erica Goodridge: Erica, thank you for immediately taking me under your wing and believing that I can achieve whatever I set out to accomplish. Thank you for giving me direction, with starting to write this book. Your great words of wisdom have truly made a great impact on my life. Thanks for being the BEST COACH AND MENTOR that a person could ever ask for. I LOVE YOU!

Intimacy With God

You cannot experience a true intimate relationship or an abundant life unless your foundation is sure. Is your foundation sure? The foundation is upon which you stand, are supported, and grounded. You wouldn't dream of moving forward without a rock solid foundation. The foundation is first, and God should be the foundation of your life. Is God first? The best way to determine whether or not God is first in your life is to ask yourself a few simple questions: What do I do with my time? Do I spend much of it praying, reading the bible, and talking to God? Or, do I spend more of it watching television and going out with friends? How is my love life with God? Do I still love God even when I don't understand Him? Or, do I draw away from Him?

An intimate relationship with God is critical. Being intimate with God, means that you are absolutely dependent on, and obedient to Him. You must depend on God for everything. Your dependence on Him should be like a child's dependence on his or her parent. As a small child, you never worried about how you would eat, what you would wear, how you would get to school each morning, or where you would live. Why not? You knew that your mother and/or father would take care of those things. They were not for a child to worry about. As an adult, your thought process must be the same. You must know that God, your heavenly Father, will do the same. He will take care of you. We must also be obedient to God. It really doesn't matter how active we may be in religious activities. What matters is how obedient we are to Him. It is impossible for one to truly serve God if he does not obey Him. Therefore, submit to God. Draw near to God so that He draws near to you. Make a commitment to Him. Say, "God, I will not do as I will, but as You will." Is this hard? Of course it is, but it's not impossible. Obedience is hard but disobedience is harder, because there is always a negative consequence to disobedience.

We write things on our heart through a combination of emotion and information. Tell God all that's on your heart. Say exactly what you are thinking. God already knows what you are thinking and the desires of your heart, but

He wants you to tell Him. If you are carrying a load that makes you anxious, unsettled, worried, fearful or disappointed, tell and release it to Him. Everyone has something going on in their life that falls short of our highest hopes. The good news is that God is always compassionate and forgiving. Therefore, we can unburden ourselves of our sorrow, our regret, our guilt, or whatever it is. Just continue to tell God that you want His way and not your way.

In many cases, we are not true. We often make broken promises. Well, I am here to tell you that God is true and will adhere to His promises. He will never make a promise and then fail to perform. Trust God and His promises, because He is still faithful, even when we are unfaithful. Ask God to "fill you with His power and anoint you with His peace."

Spend time with God. Although it isn't always easy, it's fun. The more time you spend with Him, the more established your relationship with Him will become. Spending time with God also strengthens your love, trust and faith in Him. Hebrews 11:6 says, "But without faith it is impossible to please God." God is the author and finisher of your faith. Besides, you are very special and precious to Him and He desires your fellowship. "If you are too busy for God, then it's time to change your schedule" and seek an up close, personal, and intimate relationship with Him.

1 What Is Your Purpose? How To Discover It

What is your purpose in life? Everyone has a gift because God has uniquely created each person. Do you know why you were created or why you exist? You may think that you have no purpose in life. God has a plan for every single person that no one else can fulfill. First, you will need to talk to the inventor or Creator (God) and read the owner's manual (the bible), in order to understand God and know why you exist. Each day, you should tell God that you want to know Him a little bit better and love Him a little bit more. If you know and love God more, you have just fulfilled one of the purposes in your life. You must know God's intention for you. Once you know His intention, you are no longer trying, you are applying.

Not knowing your purpose doesn't mean that you have no purpose. It simply means that, it may take more work to define it. Whether or not you believe that you have a purpose, you can still discover it. You must empty your mind of the disbelief. A lack of belief can prevent you from discovering why you were created. Why go through life without knowing your purpose? That would mean that you have missed the point. Don't miss the point. Bishop T.D. Jakes says, "When you come to the pivotal points in your life, listen for God's direction. Become acquainted with His voice, so that you will be able to distinguish the difference between His voice and your head. By hearing and obeying Him, you will move closer to the destination He has preset for you, and you will receive His abundant favor and grace."

You may be wondering, "How exactly am I supposed to define my purpose?" God didn't put you on this earth just to mark things off of your to-do list. Pastor Joel Osteen says, "You are where God wants you to be at this very moment. Every experience is part of His divine plan. Be confident and thankful that he has a special purpose for your life." Identifying and releasing your life purpose is the key to self-mastery and personal development, the essence of a full and happy life. There are many people around the world who are already living out their life purpose and enjoy a fulfilled, empowered existence every day. You can join them.

You must take steps to reveal specific insights about your own character. You must be clear about your overall context for life first. Be in tune with who you really are. In reality, how do you view life? Go to a quiet place, a place where you will not be interrupted or distracted. Turn off any home, office, or cell phone. Take out a sheet of paper and a pen and begin writing down anything that you would like to do or any goals that you wish to achieve. Think about your gifts, talents and abilities. Write them down as well. While you are thinking and writing, ask yourself these questions:

What is it that I truly love to do?

What is it that I do well?

What is it that I would do even if I didn't get paid for it?

What is my passion?

What makes me feel close to God?

What ways do I feel called to be of service to others?

What do I strongly believe in?

What is a major hardship or challenge that I have overcome?

How did I overcome the major hardship or challenge?

What makes me feel great about myself?

What do people typically ask me to help with?

What makes me smile?

What are my most important values?

How could I use my talents and gifts to help people, causes, organizations, the world, etc?

What were some of my hobbies in the past?

What are some of my hobbies in the present?

Who do I consider a role model or inspiration to me?

Why are they considered a role model or inspiration to me?

Each question and answer reflects a piece of your purpose, but they aren't complete. After writing the answers to each of these questions, prepare to write a personal mission statement. This will help you because it will require you to brainstorm and think outside of the box. Your mission statement will create a change in you because it forces you to align your behavior with your beliefs. You will also have to re-arrange your priorities. As you begin writing your mission statement, look at your questions and answers and write down any "action" words that you can relate to. For example: encourage, inspire, equip, educate, empower, etc. Afterward, write down every resource and every individual that you are almost certain can help and support you. Finally, using your action words and your support information, write out what you would like to accomplish, how or who can you use to help you with your accomplishment, and what you would like the end result to be.

You have now created your personal mission statement. Re-arrange your priorities and step out and try it. Remember, you and God are a team. When you take a step, God takes a step. While you are on your mission, you may have a feeling of needing to do something else or find an excuse to quit. The feeling of resistance will pass if you will just keep pushing and pressing forward. Sometimes it takes a life altering, eye opening experience to snap you out of your state of unconsciousness. Those experiences push you to continue to move forward. You are in a learning experience. Your purpose has great potential and your potential is not here to rest. It is here to grow.

Don't ever give up. Quitting or failure is not an option. You may not know your purpose now but as long as your heart is open, you will find God and He will find you. Listen to your inner voice. Practice listening to the voice inside of you that guides you to your true desire. Rise and be great, do the great things that you were meant to do.

Be patient and don't waste your time on things that you know aren't from God; like get rich quick schemes. Don't allow people to talk you into things. It may sound great to the world but it doesn't mean that it's God's plan for you. As your knowledge grows and deepens, you will find greater and greater opportunities for fulfilling your life's mission. When considering taking advantage of new opportunities, ask yourself, "How does this align with my goals?" If it doesn't, don't pursue it; regardless of how much money you can make. Money won't keep you committed to doing something but your passion will.

Passion+Production=Performance….People who love what they do get the best results. Search for what gives your life meaning and makes your heart sing. Know what you want, do what you love, live your passion, chase your dream, be free, stand for something, get more out of life, smile, and believe in yourself. Make your calling your work.

When you find your purpose, you will usually find that it is something that you are tremendously passionate about. Once you discover your purpose, you have to keep working at it and working on yourself, until you become that purpose. Embrace your purpose and you will discover yourself to be a greater person than you ever dreamed yourself to be. The world you live in will never be the same, and the opportunities that life will throw at you will be abundant.

2 *Growing In Integrity*

Integrity is the state of being SOUND and COMPLETE. It is the quality of being honest and adherence to high values and principles. There are elements and words used which partially describe the character of someone who has integrity.

Being **consistent** is a very important element of integrity. Be consistent with your actions and behaviors. Being one person in public and another in private leads to a disjointed life and contradicts being a person of integrity. This does not mean that everything you do in life should be publicly announced, leaving you with no private life. Everyone should have a private life. This means that a person with a disjointed life has certain beliefs but their behaviors show otherwise. Example: This person can speak against sexually exploiting children but carry on acts with child pornography. That definitely contradicts what you speak about. When others notice that you are unpredictable, they are unlikely to see you as a person who maintains integrity. Therefore, consistency is a must.

People who have integrity are **honest**. Being honest is important because there are people who put their trust and faith in you and it goes hand and hand with being honest. If you are a person who wants to grow in integrity, you will want to build good relationships with people as well. You do this by being honest with others. When you are honest, people will support, respect, and help you. Honesty is also used by others to help determine your character. Being dishonest can lead to a person never believing you again, even when you are being honest.

Growing in integrity requires you to be **truthful**. It takes much less time to tell the truth than to justify a lie. In fact, it's so much easier to remember the truth than a ton of lies. When you are truthful, you appear to be credible and people will appreciate you more. Sometimes when you make regretful mistakes, your ability to be truthful may be tested. Regardless of how hard it may be, you must eliminate being untrue or being in denial. Being untrue, goes back to people having a lack of trust in you.

Being **scrupulous** is also important while growing in integrity. As a person of integrity, you should always be very cautious in whatever you do. Doing the right things are extremely important. To keep yourself lined up and to ensure that you are thorough or paying close attention to your decision making, you must be extremely attentive and strict on yourself. A scrupulous person will always act in the best interest of themselves to avoid doing wrong.

People of integrity are **faithful**. Faithfulness is also an important element of integrity. Faithful people have consistent behavioral patterns which births their character. They are strong athletes, strong in service, strong in grace, etc...They are strong because they have a determination to show their faithfulness. Faithful people are bound to whatever they are set out to accomplish. They show steadfast loyalty. Nothing changes or moves them. Being faithful requires you to submit and be humble. This means that you must have a good attitude and behavior.

To be a person of integrity, you must be **trustworthy**. Demonstrating behaviors that build trust are extremely important. In doing so, you must become reliable and caring. This greatly aids in forming solid relationships. In order to form solid relationships, you must sustain good communication. Clear up misunderstandings so that you do not compromise trust. Always maintain realistic expectations to others to ensure that you are being trustworthy. Make trust a priority, something that you craft over a time and allow it to grow naturally. Remember that trust is a learned skill, so be compassionate with yourself in the process.

Being **principled** is another important element of integrity. Principled people have strong core values. They stand for things that are important, such as being a person of integrity. They are always looking for ways to develop their existing knowledge and continually expanding their ability to do things. Therefore, they consider learning to be a never ending process. They read the best literature to keep up with current affairs and events; while working smart, being creative and productive (all at the same time). Principled people normally radiate positive energy. They are usually active socially, have many friends and interests and maintain being cheerful, happy, and pleasant; along with having an optimistic attitude.

People of integrity are **open**. Being open includes talking about yourself. Even if that means talking about the things you did on that particular day. Talking about things you've done will show people that you are capable of communicating any and everything. Expressing yourself is also a way of being open. Expressing your opinion is important because your opinion matters to other people. Never hide your true feelings. People pick up on hiding and will never fully trust you.

People of integrity are **whole**. To be whole means to be complete. That involves all of our being. When a person is whole, they feel comfortable with themselves. Although every person always has room for improvement, a whole person is in a state of being as God has willed. They feel a sense of peace.

While growing in integrity, you must be **fair**. Fair people are not biased. They do not play favoritism and always treat everyone within reason. The rules set are the same for everyone to follow.

Now that you know some of the characteristics of a person who has integrity, I must share from a Christian perspective as well.

Integrity is a quality of life and a process of living. You are the only one who can apply integrity into your life. It is a commitment to a whole-life process of constructing and reconstructing character, which is never finished. While growing in integrity, you must have a desire to please God more than you have a desire to please yourself. You must have a working knowledge of the word of God. If you are not doing devotionals, you need to start. You should not start your day without God. Spend time with God. Get to know the word and learn how to apply it. Godly exercise is the key to Godly character. If you want an increase of Christ, there must be a decrease of self. Stop putting yourself first and using God as a spare tire when things don't go as planned. Whatever you put FIRST, governs what happens to the rest. Accept His wisdom above your own and surrender your views and opinions to Him. As soon as you start putting your focus in the right direction, things will begin shifting for the better. Remember, a change in behavior begins with a change in heart. Stop being a fan of Jesus and instead be a follower.

Repentance is very important. True repentance is more than just remorse. It involves a change of mind with no intention to go back into the other direction. Be quick to repent and confess your sins, seeking God's enabling grace to change directions. Take a good look at your conduct and consider your ways. Examine your daily walk and listen to your conscience. Pray about the daily affairs of life. Pray about where you are getting ready to go. Pray about the people you will be surrounded by all day long. You can spend your time in an attitude of prayer. Pray without ceasing. Prayer truly helps. It releases the power of heaven and changes things. The first thing that it will change is YOU.

Integrity is not something that is built in you over night. In fact, it rarely comes quickly or painlessly. You will still face struggles, but God works through our circumstances over an extended period of time. God does not desire us to fail but failure may be used to develop our Godly character. He will work in us, throughout successes and failures, teaching us important lessons about ourselves and Him as well. While working in us, He is conforming us to the image of His Son. This is an image that we should desire to be molded into for the rest of our lives.

3 <u>*Change Your Perspective*</u>

In almost any aspect of life, how we perceive things defines our reality. There's always more than one way of looking at any experience. How do you perceive your experiences? Do you find opportunity in every difficulty? Or do you find difficulty in every opportunity?

The simplest example of this is the literal one. If you look at an amusement park from a different position, you will see different things. Some things that were hidden in one view become visible in another. Some things will also be easier to recognize, from one perspective than another. Viewing an amusement park from a sky ride, gives a very different impression of the attractions at the park than viewing it from ground level. Also, viewing a presidential speech, with the television on mute, can be quite a frustrating experience. My point is that there are different and better ways to see things. Instead of complaining about not being able to hear the speech, try taking the television off of mute. Try finding ways to do things better the next time. Change your perspective!

You create your own reality. If you perceive that you have endless opportunities and that you are lining yourself up to be successful, that's what your reality will be. On the other hand, if you focus on all of your difficulties, all you get is a feeling of anxiety and frustration.

Everyone encounters problems in life and always will. The most important thing is to look at them from the right perspective. Just move some things around in your brain and they will go wherever you push them. It may take some practice, but you can do it. Changing your perspective will always help you understand a situation better and avoid false views.

Joyce Meyers says, "Look for the treasure in every trial." Develop an attitude of gratitude and give thanks for everything that happens to you; knowing that every step forward is a step toward achieving something bigger and better than your current situation. Claim that no matter where you are at or how tight it is, God is going to rescue you.

Most people have deeply held beliefs on some subjects. This can sometimes make it harder for them to look at things from another person's view point. When you look at everything from your own view point, you may often offend people, argue and find things hard to resolve. If you have a disagreement with someone, imagine yourself as the other person, and try to see how they see the situation. Recognize that there are intelligent, thoughtful, good people who have different opinions from you.

Happiness is a choice. No one can make you happy. If you complain, you remain. Pastor Joel Osteen says, "You can't change what has already happened, so choose to look ahead instead of behind you." Tell yourself, "I am in a place to undertake anything coming toward me. I can endure it." God desires for us to be confident in His character and to have a hopeful attitude, even in difficulties. Inspirational speaker, Iyanla Vanzant said, "Your willingness to look at your darkness is what empowers you to change."

Improving yourself is always an option, but how you choose to do that is entirely up to you. The power to change your life lies in you. Look in the mirror, anything you see can change. Sometimes, the best thing that you can do to change your perspective is to literally change what is right in front of you. You may have heard someone say, "When I do right, no one remembers. When I do wrong, no one ever forgets." Don't give up, keep doing right. Be determined to do right, even when others around you are doing wrong.

Although the road may appear rough and beyond repair, stop focusing on your lack. The more you dwell on what you don't have, the more you get what you don't want. Re-shift your focus on things that you have, even if they seem small. Everything that you need to fulfill your destiny is within your reach, if only you would look and focus in its direction. Feeling grateful or appreciative of someone or something in your life actually attracts more of the things that you appreciate and value into your life. APPRECIATION= GUARANTEED ATTRACTION!

Change comes with maturity. Getting older does not mean that a person is mentally maturing, but will most certainly prove that a person is physically maturing. Accept that some people will have the same perspective, mentality, and actions that they had 15-20 years ago. Mental maturity does not come with age. One must have a change in heart in order to have a change in mind. Bishop TD Jakes says, "Your past life is too small to fit you as you grow into the fullness of all you were meant to be. To hold on to it is an expression of your constant need to see all things from the small perspective of a previous experience." Let go of "PAST" mentalities and behaviors and grow into the fullness of your future.

Changing your life doesn't always mean turning your entire world upside down. Sometimes, it's just about getting a new perspective of yourself, or the world around you. Some of the benefits of changing your perspective could be:

-Feeling refreshed

-Feeling more hopeful

-Experiencing more appreciation and love

-Turning disadvantages into advantages

-Calming you down at stressful times

-Opening up new possibilities that you hadn't thought of before

-Enjoying and appreciating more

-Mending relationships

-Leading to a more satisfying life

-The ability to see other people's point of view

4 *Positive vs. Negative*

Did you know that studies show that people who express positive emotions live on average 10 years longer than people who express negative emotions? I have learned that being negative is a constant, non-stop, stressful drain on my mental, emotional and physical bandwidth. How can a person live a positive life with a negative mind? Being positive relieves stress and helps me to be less sensitive to problems, which results in less illness. When we dwell on the negative, we are releasing our faith in the wrong direction. Fill your mind with positive things, so that there is no room for the negative. Pastor Joel Osteen says, "Serve an eviction notice to the negative thoughts. Tell them that they have occupied your rooms long enough and that you have a new tenant, which is: FAITH, HOPE, VICTORY, ABUNDANCE, and INCREASE!

It often takes time to get to know someone. Therefore, you should take time to form opinions about them as well. The bible says, "Watch and pray." That does not mean to "watch and criticize, watch and gossip or watch and judge." Positive people have more friends, which is a key factor to their happiness and the length of their life. Although, you should take time forming opinions of others, you must still be cautious of people who show signs of being negative or are hard to read. When the character of a person is unclear to you, look at their friends. Are they people who make you feel welcome to be around? Are they engaging in positive activities or are they doing the exact opposite?

The most important single influence in the life of a person is another person. Keep away from people who try and belittle your ambitions. Small people always do that, but the great make you feel that you too, can become great. As the sayings go, "Hurt people, hurt people" and "Free people, free people."

You must avoid negativity in every way possible. Being around negative people and environments, eventually rub off on you (to some degree). Sometimes, you have to separate yourself from some of the people that you consider closest to you. Don't allow your status with a person (known to be negative) determine your loyalty to them. Just because you work with, grew up with, or are related to someone does not mean that you have to "mingle or click" with them. Remember, "Everything that's good to you is not always good for you." Having a negative attitude is like having a flat tire. "You won't get anywhere until you fix it."

Be original, be who you are. If you were born to stand out, why would you want to become a copy? Be careful, because those who follow the crowd, usually get lost in it. Keep in mind that some people are usually more negative than the people that they talk about. People can feel and sense when a person has a negative demeanor. Besides, if you are a negative person, people tend to avoid you and there are a number of consequences. Some of them include: **Using poor judgment-** people who use poor judgment, often act before they think. They make bad or irrational decisions and sometimes regret them when it's often too late. **Lack of self-confidence-** they don't trust themselves or others. They don't think they have the necessary skills to be successful. They often feel worthless, and have fears which hold them back from pursuing positive things.

Cluttered mind and racing thoughts- their mind is in a state of confusion. They often feel as if there are just too many things to keep up with, which could make them feel overwhelmed. They deal with tons of different thoughts and ideas that are going very fast, which could also be symptoms of having a medical condition.

Being positive allows you to think more clearly so that you are more likely to make rational decisions. You have a relaxed state of mind, which helps your alertness and your focus. It's good for inspiration and learning. Having a relaxed state of mind also helps make you feel pure and whole (or complete) and you have more belief in yourself. You have more confidence in your decision making. Have you ever noticed a person that exemplifies confidence? They have a positive attitude and a people tend to be drawn to them. Being positive helps you have a positive impact on your interaction with the people around you. Positivity lowers stress and increases your life span. It can have a positive effect on your mood and overall health.

To be positive, you have to eliminate certain negative thinking patterns. If your thoughts are negative, replace them with encouraging, realistic, and positive ones. In order to do that, you must train your mind by developing an awareness of your own thinking. Positive thinking starts with self-talk. Ask yourself (regularly) what am I thinking about right now? Other ways to train your mind are:

-**Think positive-** Encourage yourself, find encouraging, positive people to be around

-**Meditate-** Spend time alone, relax and center your thoughts

-**Read good books-** Reading forces you to use your imagination as your brain automatically pictures everything that you read

-**Each day think of good ideas-** Try new things and things that are different from what you have been doing

Break old habits and routines- Take a new route to work (sightsee). Since we know that alcohol is a depressant that slows down mental functions, stop drinking

Be a continual learner- Never stop being curious, seek new experiences, skills and knowledge. Think of something that you've always wanted to learn and get started.

Expand your vocabulary- Decide to learn a new word each day. It expands your mind and is impressive to others when you use new words.

Focus on positives ONLY- Be determined to focus on bigger, brighter and better things.

Become aware of your thoughts and make a conscious effort to notice what your inner voice is telling you. How do you want to be perceived in life? You make the decision but being positive sets you on the right track towards being successful in life.

5 _Let It Go_

Often times, you don't realize that holding onto some things, prevents you from moving forward in life. In this chapter, I will be discussing a number of things that are necessary to let go of, in order to live a healthy, happy, and more prosperous life.

In many cases, you want to be in control of EVERYTHING. That includes the lives of your children and other people's lives as well; without understanding that a controlling behavior only increases your stress and anxiety levels. It keeps you in a place of feeling fatigue, exhausted and depleted. You can never be in a relaxed state if you never choose to loosen the grip on such behavior.

There are many ways in which you can start to change that behavior. You must begin by recognizing when you are displaying a controlling behavior. You often measure people by whether or not they live up to your expectations. Cease this type of thinking and retrain your mentality. When you make a decision to let go of that, the urge to correct what others do is no longer your focus and the habit of wanting people to give in to you is less desirable. Listening to objections and disagreements of others, help you to stop using them to trigger your own opinions. By doing so, you will start to feel a great relief and your impatience begins to lessen. Your mind will give up on calculating every move in advance, which will help reduce your stress level.

Major issues that every individual must let go of are: anger, grudges and bitterness. We often hold on to these things when people we care about hurt us. The heaviest thing to carry is a grudge. We must forgive the individuals who hurt us. Forgiveness is not only possible but it's necessary for your own well-being (not for the other person's). Forgiveness does not change the past but it does "enlarge" the future. LET IT GO!

Although hurtful actions and words of other people can be wounds that leave you with feelings of resentment, and cause you to have thoughts of revenge, you must practice forgiveness. Forgiveness will lead you down a path with feelings of gratitude, joy, and hope.

Again, it does not justify the other person's wrong. It means that you are altering how you view the situation. It will help you to be more positive and at peace in your life.

Being hurt by someone you love or trust can leave you with feelings of sadness and confusion as well. You must not dwell on those situations because it can lead to high blood pressure, symptoms of depression, stress, unhealthy relationships, higher risks of alcohol and substance abuse. This is not something that you want for yourself. Letting go of hurtful events can promote positive feelings and allow you to enjoy the present. Your life has so much more meaning and purpose. You will also have very valuable friendships and relationships, while having enriching connections with others as well.

Reflect on how you have reacted in certain situations and how it may have affected your overall life. Be determined to move past the situation in a positive manner. Doing so will help you move away from your role as a victim and release the control and power that the offending person had in your life. It will also help you to find compassion and understanding.

The people who are the hardest to love are the ones who need it the most. LOVE THEM ANYWAY!

Being around or in an environment with people who hurt you may present some discomfort. You may begin to feel stressed or tense. Keep in mind that you can always choose to attend or avoid specific functions. Always be willing to allow certain experiences to help you move forward by keeping an open heart and mind.

Don't wait for an apology. Remember, this is an internal process, something that you are doing for yourself. Make a decision today to be honest with yourself by recognizing and admitting to your grudges. Finally, say goodbye to them. Some people don't even know why you are carrying a grudge against them because it's probably been so long. Tell your grudges that they will no longer fester and destroy your peace of mind. You will no longer be miserable and suffering. You will spend your energy focusing on happier things in life. LET THEM GO!

Sometimes you hold onto friendships and relationships that are physically and mentally draining, which can also be contributing factors to high levels of stress. You must be willing to let go of these situations by eliminating the friendships and relationships. In many cases, you are trying to mend and hang on to something that is already gone. You often hold onto things that used to be so wonderful because you fear losing a person and being alone. You must let go of things and people of the past, and begin to learn how to live with your current state of being. There is a saying that says, "Some things that we do are like feathers in the wind, we can't get it all back." That is so true. You can't always get a person to love and care for you the way they did when you first met them. They no longer have the same feelings of the past and in many cases, "neither should you."

Have you ever noticed that when you have just made a decision in life and have come to the point of changing some people, places, and things (because you know it's necessary), satan comes along and reminds you of the "remember whens, what ifs, buts and maybes?" He then destroys your plan to let go. As much as you hate to, you start all over, try it again, and end with the same results. Feelings of hurt, pain, betrayal and rejection return. Joyce

Meyers says, "You can't tell the devil to get out, if at the same time you're opening the door to let him back in." LET IT GO!

The importance of letting go is to have more clarity. We see reality as it really is. Being in denial or denying the truth does not make it go away. Be aware of the NOW and you will discover what is real today. When you let go, you have more time to be happy and enjoy what you have along with yourself. The only way to be truly happy is to accept and value who you are and what you have. Every person should desire to have more enjoyable experiences in life, and letting go is the only way to move forward and do exactly that.

Letting go also enhances your intuition. You can clearly receive and be in the moment. It will increase your energy as well. It eliminates your mind from being two places at once (which is often very tiring) and allows more energy to flow. Make a decision to let go of the past, which was fun. "Fun is temporary but joy is eternal." Claim a better tomorrow and live a joyful life!

6 *KNOW YOUR SELF-WORTH*

Do you sometimes feel worthless? Have you ever felt disappointed for not achieving certain goals that you had placed a deadline on? Do you question your value or your self- worth? Do you know your self-worth? Knowing your self-worth is based on whether or not you have a healthy self-esteem. If you answered yes to any of the questions above, you may need to discover ways to develop and boost your self-esteem.

In order to have a better appreciation of your own self-worth, you must recognize that there is a need for growth and change. What do you see when you look at yourself? Do you like what you see when you look at yourself? Do you see a person of integrity and good character? Do you see a person who values themselves? If not, then you need to work on improving your self-esteem.

Strive to think positive thoughts at all times. In order to do so, you must eliminate all negative self-talk. A major part of improving you self-esteem is to monitor the things that you say to yourself and others. Speak positive things that would be a positive influence in your life. When you think and speak positive, you are making a deposit into your self-worth bank. When you speak negative, you are making a withdrawal from your self-worth bank. Which one do you want? Sometimes things don't always go as planned and will seem to be falling apart, but if you block all of the negative out and begin to think positive, it will all come together. Don't allow negative thoughts to cause you to fall into a state of misery.

Often, we feel this sense of discouragement based on other people's judgment and opinions of us. We hear things so many times that we accept it as the truth. It's always best to "Manage the opinions of others. " We should never value the opinions of others more than our own. Too often, we allow people with no proven leadership to change our thinking. Remember, "What you listen to leads you."

Never open the door to allow others to influence the way you think. If you do this, you will operate on auto pilot. Smart people think for themselves. It has been said that "A person who does not think for their self, does not think at all." You have your own mind. Use it to the best of your ability.

People often say and do things that are negative to others because they feel as if they can. Their negative behavior has been accepted because the other person does not know their own worth. This is the case in many relationships with mates, parents, family, friends, and co-workers. Limit the amount of time that you spend with people of that type. Choose to completely surround yourself with positive and inspiring influences. You will feel much happier and better about yourself if you do.

You can be happy and you are worth it. Be confident and comfortable with yourself. Those who lack self-confidence, often brag and falsely talk themselves up to other people. Enjoy your own company. You are the greatest love that you will ever have in your life. Love and befriend yourself, and watch the quality of your life improve.

So many people are happy on Valentine's Day. Well, what about the day after and every day going forward? What happens when all of the nice gifts are gone? Will you still feel the excitement? Will you still care or feel cared about? The words, "I love you," have become just a figure of speech for many. If a person loves another person, "EVERYDAY" should be Valentine's Day to them. Love is an "action," not just a feeling. Remember, LOVE DOES NOT HURT MENTALLY, PHYSICALLY OR EMOTIONALLY. Learn to love every day.

Self-esteem is concerned with the way we judge our own worth. Having low self-esteem is overwhelming and often goes hand and hand with stress and depression. Do you have the ability to look upon yourself as having value? It's surprising how quick we are to accept another person's judgment, over our own. You can be the nicest person, have the best parents, be the smartest kid in the school, and have the best friends; but somehow, another person's negative opinion of you has caused you to believe otherwise.

How you look or dress does not dictate your level of self-esteem. It's dictated by your ability to look upon yourself as having value. Having money in your bank account does not validate you. A person who knows their self-worth may not drive the finest car, live in the finest home, or wear the finest clothes but are always on their feet prepared and ready to face any challenge with unshakeable confidence. No, they are not arrogant, but there is an air about them that people can't help but notice when they walk into a room.

People will have expectations of you, but you cannot become too focused on what or who others want you to become. Don't try living to their standards. BE YOURSELF! Focus on what will make you happy. Discover what it is that you want to do with your life. Ask yourself, "What could I do that would make me really happy in life? Allow your imagination to soar to all of the different possibilities. Don't allow others to tell you that you are not being realistic. Don't allow fear to hinder you from pursuing what truly makes you happy. F.E.A.R.= False Evidence Appearing Real. Real happiness comes from being content with and proud of yourself. Don't allow worrying and belittling yourself to cause you to miss out on the happiness that could be in store for you. Focus on what will make you happy.

Everyone is different, and have their own unique qualities and talents. Figure out your qualities or special gifts that will set you apart from everyone else. Your mission should be to create a reason for existing. Once you have figured it out, start believing yourself and pressing forward immediately. Now that you know what you want in life, write out a clear goal that you have in mind and be specific. Be sure to avoid procrastination, because it will kill your dreams. Last but not least, have faith and spend a little time each day envisioning yourself with all that you desire. Make it seem perfectly real in your mind and take note of what events happen to bring you to that point.

Below are some encouraging and inspiring quotes. Make a copy and put them where you can see them each day:

-We are each gifted in a unique and important way. It is our privilege and our adventure to discover our own special light. ~Mary Dunbar

-You gain strength, courage and confidence by every experience in which you really stop to look fear in the face. ~Eleanor Roosevelt

-Don't you dare, for one more second, surround yourself with people who are not aware of the greatness that you are. ~Jo Blackwell-Preston

-Yours is the energy that makes your world. There are no limitations to the self except those you believe in. ~Jane Roberts

-Your chances of success in any undertaking can always be measured by your belief in yourself. ~Robert Collier

-To be beautiful means to be yourself. You don't need to be accepted by others. You need to accept yourself. ~Thich Nhat Hanh

-You are very powerful, provided you know how powerful you are. ~Yogi Bhajan

-You yourself, as much as anybody in the entire universe, deserve your love & affection. ~Buddha

-Of all the judgments we pass in life, none is more important than the judgment we pass on ourselves.
~Nathaniel Branden

-People are like stained-glass windows. They sparkle and shine when the sun is out, but when the darkness sets in their true beauty is revealed only if there is light from within. ~Elisabeth Kübler-Ross

-"Self-worth comes from one thing – thinking that you are worthy".~ Wayne Dyer

-"When you please others in hopes of being accepted, you lose you self-worth in the process".~ Dave Pelzer

-"To be yourself in a world that is constantly trying to make you something else is the greatest accomplishment". ~Ralph Waldo Emerson

7 _Become A Better You_

Becoming a better person is an ongoing process. You can be one of the best people, but there is always room to be better. Therefore, it's important that you make growing a daily habit. Becoming a better person requires growth. Choose to grow. Believe in your mind that there is room for growth and that you will not limit yourself from doing so. Many things that have taken place in our lives did not happen overnight and cannot be expected to change overnight. Growth is a process, as well and results are not always instant. It will not make you a perfect person, but it will surely help you to become a happier person.

If you don't like who you have become, make a decision to work on becoming a better person. Identify any negative traits that you dislike about yourself, and work on them one by one. It may be challenging but it's possible. Take responsibility for your life. You are the only person who can change it. No one else can do it for you. Blaming other people or conditions for your life is not good. In every situation (good or bad), you are the person who makes the decision of how to respond to it and how it will affect you.

Develop good habits that will help you grow. Do something consistently every day, even if it's something small. Just doing small things can make a big difference over time. Begin to feed your mind with things of quality. You can choose to pray, meditate, read, listen and watch inspirational and motivational materials. They are always great ways to growing and becoming better. As long as you are being consistent, growth will be in store for you.

Always practice good etiquette. Show that you have good manners by always saying things like, "excuse me, please, thank you and you're welcome." Good etiquette goes a long way and helps you attract more of the same.

Commit to continuously learning. Learning goes far beyond going to pre-school to graduating from a college or university. Learning is a life-long personal development task. In order to become the best you can be, you must add learning and being creative to your daily agenda in order to consistently improve yourself. Never feel as though you are "good enough." The best never think that way.

Better equip yourself with skills. The more skills you have, the more you can help yourself and others as well. Strengthen your current skills and continue to learn. Regardless of how much you know, there are always new things to learn. Have a thirst for knowledge, so you will continue to increase it. Be sharp, and develop your observation skills. Sharp people are usually the first to catch on to things because they are often thinking ahead of others. These skills can help you be a better and more attractive member to your community, a better human to others and a better person in the world. You can be helpful by becoming involved in different interest groups, recreational clubs and making the world a better place.

You are greatly influenced by the people around you. Stay surrounded by people who act as a positive source of energy and inspiration for you. Role models are great examples for inspiration and make it easier for you to achieve something. They have many positive traits that you desire, and are concrete examples of who and what you want to be. Act as if you are already who you want to become, today. Another key to becoming a better you, is to find a mentor. Remember, you cannot be the smartest person in your circle. There will be no opportunity for growth for you if you are the smartest. Unlike role models, you have a personal relationship with your mentor and they can help you grow much faster by helping to guide you through the walk of life.

Be a role model to others. Do your best to be an inspirational guide to others. This includes being a better friend, sibling, partner, parent, employee, etc. We often make such expectations of others, so we need to focus on meeting that same expectation. Decide to treasure your family and loved ones. You are extremely fortunate to have them. There are many who only wish that they did.

It's easy to make demands and expectations but difficult to take ownership for the things that we should be doing but aren't. For example, many of us complain about the wages and benefits of our jobs. We complain of not having enough or it's just not good enough. Have you ever really thought about how you can be a better employee? Is there anything more that you can do for your manager? Are there any new projects that you can take on? Is there any possible way that you can improve your current performance? On the other hand, as a manager, you should commit to finding ways to retain employees by focusing on increasing their motivation levels. Have you thought about putting their needs before yours, to bring out the best in them?

There are so many things that you can do to become a better you. One important process to doing so is to always have the best intentions for others. Reach for the highest levels in everything that you do and think. While it is definitely important to be bold and assertive, not living in fear, and standing up for what you believe in; it's equally important to be attentive, caring, compassionate, and kind. When others are talking, give them your full attention. Show them that you care. That usually makes them feel good. Don't be so caught up in your own self that you can't see the needs of others.

Lend a helping hand. The smallest bit of help is very much appreciated by others. Make it a habit to consider others. Instead of finding their weaknesses, look at what they are good at and recognize their strengths. Be trusting. Remember that the baseline intention of people is usually good. Usually their wrong doing come from lacking. Avoid being rude to others because everyone has feelings and we should be sensitive to them.

Be adventurous, step out and do things that you've never done. Doing so will broaden your perspective and widen your horizon. When a person broadens their perspective, it helps them to be more accepting of differences with others. Every person is different and differences add variety and color into our lives. It also helps us to be more versatile when necessary. Being able to adapt to different situations make you so much more powerful than the one who is rigid.

Do the best you can to exercise your judgment appropriately. Always carefully evaluate everything you are given before accepting it. This way you can be more open to challenging yourself to take on more of the things that you have never done. Increase your capacity by stretching yourself. While you are holding yourself to the highest standard in everything you do, you should always use good judgment and be aiming for excellence. In closing, I would like to encourage you to be persistent, never give up and be determined to become a better you, regardless of what it looks or feels like.

Below are some words used to describe people who work to become better:

Empathetic
      Optimistic

Trustworthy
      Merciful

Generous
      Accepting

Sensitive
      Independent

Forgiving
      Peaceful

Loving
      Integrity

Fair
      Nurturing

Respectful
      Helpful

Disciplined
      Moral

Strong
      Grateful

Wise
      Hardworking

Reasonable
      Sharing

Understanding
      Humble

Patient
      Friendly

Gentle   Courteous

            Dependable   Thoughtful

Coachable   Committed

            Changed

8 *Move Away From Your Comfort Zone*

Leaving your comfort zone can be scary but may end up being good. Sometimes we know that we need to do things differently but our lack of self-motivation prevents us from doing so. In many cases, we must be forced by an unexpected, life changing event in order to move away from what is familiar and comfortable to us. Usually when this happens, we become extremely frightened. We fail to realize that we may be open to new and exciting opportunities that we always wanted to try.

So many people are unhappy with their jobs and their current living situation but have become complacent. They live day after day, unhappy just because they don't know how to move away from their comfort zone. Suddenly, the company they worked at for many years had a massive downturn in the industry and they lost their job. They were devastated and never thought anything like that could happen to them. The end result can often be that their lives would be thrown into a path of change, which could possibly reward them.

In many cases, losing a job forced some people to look for self-employment. Some turned to the internet. There were some who involved themselves in every internet opportunity that they could find and only made a few dollars. There were others who soon realized that they could make more money with an internet business than they had been making on their high paid jobs. The more successful people researched the market to determine a demand for the product before buying into it.

If you want a more rewarding life, you must push yourself out of your usual routine. You must take chances and risks. Staying in your comfort zone, are all familiar with the "focus on your strengths" motto. Little do we know, we will learn very little with that type of thinking. In order to gain new skills, we must try new activities that will allow us to have new experiences. Guts and determination will help us face our challenges, while gaining as well.

Moving away from something that we are so used to, can leave us with mixed emotions. We anticipate it for months, maybe even years. In many cases, new beginnings start with unfamiliar surroundings and a new environment. We want to stay because we feel safe. At the same time, we know that having new surroundings could possibly show us something much bigger and brasher than us. Do you want a change? Do you want a sense of clarity? Do you want a feeling of enlightenment? Will you take advantage of the opportunity when you are presented with it?

Don't worry about who will or won't understand you. Don't worry about feeling lonely. If you would just push yourself to keep going until something interesting happens, you will begin to see differently. These feelings are mostly about your state of mind. Change your mindset. Don't put a barrier around your mind. Be open to exploring new people, places, and things. When you do this, you will begin to lose track of all of the worry.

Procrastination will often keep you from moving away from your comfort zone. Stop waiting until you get in a better position. Most of the time, the better position never comes until you create it. So, "quit hanging on the handrails." Let go, surrender and go for the ride of your life. DO IT EVERYDAY! You must be able to differentiate "waiting and procrastinating."

Abraham Lincoln once said, "Good things come to those who wait but only what's left from those who hustle." Sometimes we drag our feet so long. While successful people are making it happen and going after the whole loaf, average people are waiting around for the crumbs. Stop waiting, cross the start line and keep moving forward! After all, you only live once but once is enough, if you do it right.

Shift your focus away from familiar patterns and habits. It's important that you expand your comfort zone. In order to do so, you must let go of living life the same way and stop rejecting change. People, who recognize that change is not only necessary, but can be good as well, usually adapt to new situations rapidly. Although there is usually a rejection of some level required, they understand that new environments can offer self- improvement. They are making major changes to their lives to fulfill a calling, a dream, or a passion.

Even if what you do works for you, trying something new could benefit you more. Decide to stop being ordinary and getting the same ordinary results. Decide to do something totally out of the ordinary, in order for you to get extraordinary results. It will not come naturally. You will have to take action in order to make the transition, but you will see your goals and desires change along the way.

The first step is always the most difficult. Therefore, breaking the task into smaller steps will lead you down your path to your goal. This usually results in success, because you are gradually building comfort, while reinforcing and internalizing the experience.

If you are shy, get out and talk to other people. You'd be surprised of what you can find out from others. Especially if it's with someone who has a path that you would like to emulate. Talking to others can help you to find out how other people achieve what you want to achieve, with a high level of success.

Sometimes you wonder why you only perform at a level of mediocrity, failing to realize that it's because your growth has become stunted. You must have a determination to move past your limited patterns of living by beginning to move forward.

Are you wondering why you are feeling stagnant in your career, or your personal or academic life? Although you have a feeling of dissatisfaction, you somehow believe that you have reached your potential. That feeling may exist because your comfort zone has become uncomfortable. Don't continue to allow your growth to be slowed down. You'd be surprised how much growth that small lateral moves can bring about in your life. Staying in your comfort zone are often patterns that inhibit growth.

We must find ways to step outside of our accustomed environments and routine way of living. Have you ever wondered to yourself, "Why am I still here, this is so uncomfortable?" It's because it's what you are used to and regardless of the level of discomfort, you stay. This same behavior pattern carries over into many other aspects of your life. A fear of letting go and moving forward has set in. You're afraid to let go of the crutch, although you don't like it. You must surrender to fear.

Oftentimes we end up in situations because of other people's expectations of us. As much as we are ready to move forward, it seems as if someone else is holding us back. Truthfully, they can only do what we allow them to do. We allow the same things to go on in our life on a daily basis. Why? It's because, we have become so used to certain situations.

For example: Many people are very unhappy in their relationships, family, and home life. Although they know that in some cases the situation is destructive, they still find it difficult to walk away. The comforts of the family unit and the family bonds keep them locked in. Often they don't think that their family would support them making a decision to change their situation. Therefore, they remain in uncomfortable and unhealthy living conditions. You must find the courage to push past it. Experience the benefits that are in store for you by soaring to higher levels.

9 *Don't Allow Life To Get In The Way*

Don't let life get in the way of you achieving your goals. Often, when you feel like you are finally moving toward success; problems, issues, and conflict always seem to arise. That is just a part of life and there will always be an opportunity for things to come in between your efforts to grow and do better. You must master handling the stumbling blocks.

Keep your eye on the prize. Avoid getting too upset about things that simply aren't worth it and are simply out of your control. Ask yourself, "Is this really a big deal?" You must determine how important the issue really is. Is it worth you losing out on a huge business deal over the fact that your car broke down? Sometimes, we don't realize how much closer life's issues can move us toward success. So remember, not to allow distractions to prevent you from doing so.

We often allow our problems or conflicts with others, cause us to lose focus and get off track. In many cases when we are upset about something dealing with another person, we often assume things. Whether we want to admit it or not, most of our assumptions are incorrect. Assumptions only escalate things more. The only way to find out the truth is to ask questions that will lead you to the facts of the matter.

Don't try dealing with all of your issues at one time. When you are trying to deal with too many things at once, you often end up solving absolutely nothing. Stick to one thing and see it through to understand before dealing with something else. This will help you avoid trying to balance too many things on your plate at once.

If you are having a problem, be solution oriented. Recognize the problem but don't focus on it. Approach the issue with the idea of working on a solution. Ask, "What can I do to fix this?" The goal is to find a way to resolve it, not to keep it continually going. Vision yourself overcoming some of your toughest challenges and achieving your goals. Doing so actually helps make your issue more personal and keeps you from going over the top.

Expecting to go through life without any problems is very unrealistic. Pastor Rick Warren says, "Life is a series of problems, you are in one now, you're just coming out of one, or you're

getting ready to go into another one."
That statement is so very true. Failure is a given in life and trying to avoid it will prevent you from obtaining what you need to cope and bounce back from it. "Failure is success turned inside out." Most successful people in the world have failed a number of times. They overcame failure and pushed through to even more success than expected.

Expect mistakes. Mistakes allow opportunity for personal growth, and helps create balance in your life. Making mistakes does not make you a failure. It happens to everyone, including the best. If you try and you fail, that's much better than never trying. No person is perfect and don't allow wanting to be a perfectionist hold you back from growing and moving further in life. You cannot succeed if you never try or never expect mistakes.

You are good enough to overcome whatever comes your way. You are good enough to be very successful. Most of the times people fail, because they quit before they even really get started. The difference between successful people and unsuccessful people is that successful people don't allow life's issues and failures to keep them down. Although they often feel inadequate, they keep trying and never give up. They have a level of determination that keeps them pressing forward.

When you are trying to recover from issues, it's important to take your time. Taking your time doesn't mean to drag your feet. It means that you are preparing to do it better the next time. In many cases, there was a process that got you to the failure point. Well, considering the fact that you did not get into most failures overnight, it will not change overnight. There is a recovery process as well.

Stop worrying and start laughing. Yes, other people will have their own views and opinions of you. Often, their criticism reflects their own inadequacies, "not yours." They have no clue of what effort has gone into what you've done and what you're trying to achieve. Choose not to feed into their negativity. Center yourself around caring people who enjoy your company and make you laugh. Worrying doesn't change things, but laughing can be an important part of your healing process.

Failures can teach you great things. Failures can be a stepping stone to a stronger you. It can teach you "what not to do" in your future. Take away a lesson from failure that's so valuable, to inform your future direction. Allow yourself to press through your failures, going above and beyond what you know. Discover new talents and find "the best in you."

Don't allow distractions to get in the way of your success by controlling your life. Be persistent, work hard, and your distractions will not keep you from being successful. Distractions often make you fearful of trying. Successful people are usually the ones who have been trying and failing and try again, many times over. Embrace fear, so that you may be released from its control.

Be determined to be strong, even when you don't know your own strength. You never know how much strength you have until you run into a mountain. Even though things appear to be falling apart, stand strong, so better things can fall together. You must fight through the bad in order to get to the good. Joyce Meyers says, "Avoid self-pity, because you can be pitiful or powerful, but you can't be both." Which would you like to be?

Turn your wounds into wisdom. Confront your issues if you want them to change, even if you feel rejected. Remember, rejection isn't meant to harm you. It's meant to arm you with the knowledge that you need to move into your destiny, but you must be consistent with your efforts. You must stop operating on convenience. You cannot just try whenever you are in a good mood. You must try at all times. Don't use time as an excuse. We each have the same amount of time in a day. Successful people make the time. You can either make the time to accomplish your goals or make excuses but again, "you can't do both." If you want what successful people have, you have to model what successful people do.

Remember, mistakes and failures are lessons and they can help you expand your existing knowledge. Don't let them hold you back. You are in control of your life and will create your own destiny. If you are passionate about something, pursue it. Be creative, and pursue what you have always allowed fear to keep you away from. Walk away from fear and seek your opportunity. Take the initiative to get things moving. It may not be easy but it's possible. Making great accomplishments is hard work, but it's often worth it in the end. MAKE IT HAPPEN!

10 *If You Close Books, You Close Opportunities*

Reading is the key to development. As a child, you were probably often told by your teachers and parents that reading is important. Also, you probably never understood or even cared to understand why. It probably never dawned on you, how necessary it was until you entered adulthood.

Reading is a life-long skill. Reading is something that you "must" do for the rest of your life. Outside of speaking, almost everything communicated is written. Regardless of what type of job you have, you will always be faced with reading, starting with the job application. If you drive, you must read highway and road signs. If you shop, you have to read labels. If you live on your own, you have to open and read the bills. Regardless of how much you dislike reading, it cannot be avoided. It's a way to access information. It's also a crucial skill in being able to function in today's society.

The more mature you become and the more you seek to grow and advance, the ability to read well becomes even more important. This is true from school age to adulthood. Your nursery rhyme books turn into text books; which equals tests and exams.

Being a good reader opens opportunities to increase your vocabulary. You often learn more vocabulary words than the average individual. Reading exposes you to words over and over again, which often makes you a successful speller. Being a good reader also helps you develop into a good writer. The more developed you are in reading, the more developed you will be overall.

Are you seeking to develop new things? Would you like to develop a good self-image? If so, start reading more. It will start to develop your mind and your imagination. If you become a good reader, you will be successful at self-educating yourself on anything that may be of interest to you. Motivation speaker, Jim Rohn says, "Formal education will make you a living; self-education will make you a fortune." Don't wait for someone else to teach you, teach yourself.

Many people are a part of online social networking groups. Being a part of these groups allow you to find people that you haven't connected with in years, opens doors for business opportunities, etc. Many of the people read and make posts throughout the course of each day. You can definitely believe that they notice your spelling and grammar. If you are looking to attract employers or even friends, you better sharpen up your reading skills; to ensure that your spelling is accurate.

Having good reading skills will also help you to have high opinions of yourself and your abilities. It gives you a feeling of having it altogether; while making you feel good about being able to take advantage of opportunities, when they are presented. Reading can be inspiring and can lead you to life changing information that you may have never envisioned possible. It makes you feel more confident, which helps build your self-esteem.

Did you know that good reading skills are vital in finding a good job? Most people who do not read well are not selected for a well-paying job. You must have good reading and comprehension skills to perform. Higher paying jobs usually require that you do special projects and reports. You will always be limited in what you can accomplish if you don't read well.

Reading is important, because it forces you to use your brain and develops the mind. In order to understand what you read, you must concentrate and focus on what you are reading. When doing so, you are exercising your mind, which is a muscle. You are helping it to grow in its ability, which results in you becoming a better listener as well. Becoming a better listener helps you to reason, understand and communicate things which are unfamiliar to you.

Have you ever wondered why you have a difficult time remembering things that you have read about in the past? Maybe it's because you haven't been reading, which helps to stretch your memory muscle and requires you to remember; if you are reading on a consistent basis. Commit to reading at least fifteen to twenty minutes daily, and watch you develop and increase your memory along with discipline.

Reading is fundamental to functioning. It's very concerning to think that there are people who can't read the instructions on their prescription sheet from the pharmacy. How can a person dream of being a homeowner if they can't read any of the agreement or closing documents? That can truly become a fearful and frustrating experience.

Many people sit around their homes complaining of being bored. If this is so, why not just pick up a magazine or a book and start reading? It won't hurt to expose yourself to new or unfamiliar words. It will only help to build your vocabulary. If you don't know the meaning of one word, you can read the context of the other words in the sentence. This will most likely help you to figure out the meaning or definition of the unknown word.

Whether you read fiction or non-fiction books, your horizon will definitely be widened. Fiction books normally seem to be more interesting or exciting but, non-fiction has the benefit of yielding long term knowledge. Non-fiction will give you more insight on diversity, how people actually live, and their customs. Being able to communicate and converse, about how others live in different parts of the world;

will prove that you are developing beyond the regular, everyday information.

If you are a reader, the possibilities for you are endless. You don't have to rely on what others tell you. You are always in a position to confirm what you have been told. You can do your own research and thinking. Reading is a building block to life.

Below are some quotes about reading:

"Not every reader is a leader, but every leader must be a reader." ....Harry Truman

"Today a reader, tomorrow a leader."....Margaret Fuller

"The more that you read, the more things you will know. The more that you learn the more places you'll go."...Dr. Suess

"A home without books is a body without soul."....Marcus Tullius Cicero

"The worth of a book is to be measured by what you can carry away from it." ....James Bryce

"A capacity and taste for reading gives access to whatever has already been discovered by others."....Abraham Lincoln

"The habit of reading is the only enjoyment in which there is no alloy; it lasts when all other pleasures fade.".... Anthony Trollope

"Reading is a basic tool in the living of a good life."....Morimer J Adler

"The man who does not read good books has no advantage over the man who can't read them."....Mark Twain

"Reading is to the mind what exercise is to the body."....Richard Steele

"What we become depends on what we read after all of the professors have finished with us.".... Thomas Carlyle

11 <u>*Create Your Own Future*</u>

Only you can decide how your future will be, so why not create a great one? Have you ever wondered why some people are successful and others are not? The reason is, because successful people have re-aligned their priorities. They made a decision to sacrifice "pleasure for opportunity." Successful people understand that they must "Give up, to go up." They shine their own light and follow their own path. If you are determined enough to turn on your light, you shall shine as well.

The first thing that you should consider is, to establish goals and write them down. It's not required to have goals in life but it makes perfect sense. The trouble with not having a "GOAL" is that you can spend your life running up and down the field and never "SCORE." Your current is determined by your past and your future is determined by your present. Take action today.

When establishing your goals, you must be objective and realistic. Successful people plan exactly what they want. **These are some of the things that they determine:**

How long it will take?

What do I need in order to accomplish the goal?

About how long should it take me to complete it?

Is this important enough to make a difference?

When is my expected completion date?

These are considered S.M.A.R.T. goals. S.M.A.R.T. goals are **S**pecific, **M**easurable, **A**ttainable, **R**elevant and **T**imely. As you grow and expand, you will develop the attitude, abilities, and skills. These will make your goals become closer and easier to attain.

Always track your goals. Successful people are always assessing their progress. They make sure that they always know what needs to be done in order to move forward. They avoid tracking things that have no bearing on achieving their goals. Successful people desire to be productive, not busy. Anyone can be busy, but it doesn't mean that you are productive. There are more people in the world who are busy than productive. You should only be tracking things that directly relate to achieving your goals. If you fail to track your progress, how can you control whether or not you meet your goals? Start tracking immediately and create graphs as well, so that you can visualize your progress.

Focus on constantly making improvements in every area of your life. Take a hard look at your present life and commit to taking one step at a time to improving it. Small steps are easier. Small positive changes make a huge difference. The more change you see, the more excited you will become about your life. Positive change gives you motivation to take on challenges that you have always desired. It gives you hope and will make you more optimistic about reaching the level of success that you aspire to. Positive changes will lead you to greatness.

Don't focus on what you did yesterday. You cannot build your future on the past. It's what you are doing today that will impact your future. Focus on where you want to be and where you are headed, not where you came from. Your past has no future, leave it behind.

You must also be careful of what you expose yourself to. Eliminate all negative thinking because your thoughts truly influence your future. Look at yourself in a positive manner. Train your mind to have good thoughts of yourself. Avoid allowing other people's thoughts and talk to affect the way you think. Evaluate the quality of what you listen to, including music. It can all play a great role in having an influence on your life; whether or not it's positive or negative. Did you know that whatever enters your mind, exits out into your life? Some people don't realize that even too much exposure to television, has a major effect on your future. You must discipline yourself by reducing your exposure to music and television that's not so healthy for you. Start allocating more time to devotions, family, reading, etc.

Take control of yourself and your environment. Learn to attract good people, ideas, and opportunities. Remember, "Your life will never be better than the average of the people you associate with." Build good friendships and relationships, in all areas of life. Be a good person and expand your network of people for the better. Your character says the most about who you are and successful people associate themselves with like-minded, sharp, and focused people. They connect to people who have their best interest at heart, and create positive energy when they are around them. Hang around people who will make a positive difference in your life.

Be ambitious! Regardless of how difficult it may be trying to accomplish what you aspire to be, keep pushing forward. You must have a strong level of determination to create your own future. Don't allow your future to be given to you. You have complete control over your life and your ambition will play a vital role in your future success.

Live a life full of expectation. Expect to move to the highest levels. Start by being consistent in your actions. Commit to doing at least one positive thing each day. Doing so will make it a positive or good habit. While developing that habit, you will start to become more disciplined. Being disciplined is a very important key to success; while it also helps to create balance in your life. You must have balance in order to be successful; while at the same time, taking action. The more action you take, the more your future will begin to look like you want it to.

Sometimes, things won't always go as planned or expected. It's still up to you to make the best of the situation. Speak life into the situation and make sure that whatever you speak or do, lines up with your goals. Keep in mind that unwanted situations will happen, but it's not about the situation; it's about how you handle it. Don't get yourself stuck in a situation too long. Accept it, handle it, and move on.

Stay on your course and you will eventually achieve your goals. Even if you are not the best at what you are doing, consistency and practice will make you better. The more you do it, the closer you will come to arriving at your final destination. Success never happens overnight. It's a process which requires much patience and practice.

You should always know when you have achieved your goals. If you have a vision which has turned into a reality, you then know that you have been successful at achieving your goals. After doing so, you should always continue on to the next level and continue to build on your success. Continue to dream and think big, while following through to the end.

Finally, acknowledge your hard work and accomplishments. Find a way to celebrate your success. After all, you have worked very hard and it's well deserved. You have made your mark, so you know that all things are possible. There is nothing to doubt and nothing to fear. You have now been successful at creating your own future!

12 *Dream It, Believe It, and Achieve It*

Have you ever dreamed of being more than just an average person? Can you vision being free to live a life of your choice? Well, I would like to let you know that you can. You can live any lifestyle that you choose because it's totally your choice. First, you must find out exactly what you want in life. Second, you must be determined to pursue your dream by immediately taking action. Be confident and take pride in knowing that you can achieve whatever you set out to accomplish, as long as you are willing to take the necessary action to do so.

Vision your success while believing it. You must shift any negative thoughts of failure to positive thoughts of success. Keep in mind that "success is failure turned inside out." Every successful person knows that, and you must believe in your heart and mind that failure is not an option for you. Although success is not an easy process, failure is an opportunity to reach success. It's only temporary. Besides, "there is no success without failure." BELIEVE IT!

Now that you have determined what you would like to accomplish and believe that you can, put on your thinking caps. Think of as many sharp individuals that may be able to help you. So often, people try to achieve their goals alone. WRONG ANSWER! Trying alone is inefficient and leads to failure. When you receive help from others, they can bring a lot of great insight, wisdom, and clarity to a situation. Thinking collaboratively could result in great reward. You may also be able to achieve your goals at a much faster pace. So, start thinking beyond yourself.

Once you have reached out to others that you would like to be on your team, tell them what it is that you would like to accomplish and ask them what their thoughts are and how they may be able to help you. You will find that some of them will have ideas that had never come across your mind. Others will be able to help you create strategic plans, focus, move out of your comfort zone, find solutions, and see the big picture of things.

Often times, people don't accomplish what they would like to because they have not laid out any specific plan of action or steps to help them. Successful people organize their goal process by setting dates and deadlines. They incorporate setting up daily reminders to complete necessary steps. They understand that programming requirements into their schedule will help them accomplish more goals concurrently.

Setting and tracking your goals will help you work smarter as opposed to working harder. The truth is that although people want to live the life of their dreams, they want time freedom even more. What good is having your dream home if you are working two jobs and overtime to keep it? What good is having a beautiful yacht docked at the beach if you can never find enough time to sail? You really need the time freedom to do it! Therefore, it is very important that you implement a plan that will work for you. You can obtain anything that you desire.

Also, Success requires an effort. There will be NO SUCCESS WITHOUT WORK! You must take action in order to be successful. Victory cannot be achieved in your comfort zone. You must reject the "usual routine" and do things that you have never done before. Positive results will only come from change. If your goal is to lose weight, you cannot continue the daily routine of eating cookies, ice cream, cakes, and snacks. You must eliminate or replace those things with healthier foods, such as fruits and vegetables. If you are a person who loves to play golf during your free time, you will need to consider exchanging golf playing with reading and doing research on how to achieve your goals in life. Successful people always sacrifice pleasure for opportunity. They are not always looking to have fun. They understand that the end result of their success, will afford them the opportunity for pleasure.

Passion and determination is also very important. Having a passion and determination for something will always keep you more focused and motivated. If you don't have a great level of passion and determination, motivational speakers and seminars will only keep the excitement going for the moment. You may feel great about what you just learned or the information that you just heard. You may experience this feeling of greatness all week long, but eventually it begins to fade away. Your motivation begins to decrease and your excitement level is on the decline. That is because you either don't have a passion for what you want to do or you are not as determined as you should be. When you have both, you can start where you are motivation-wise and continue from there. Being passionate and determined will keep your mind full of ideas and thoughts, which leads to action. The constant action will increase your motivation. When you reach this level, you will notice that your lunch breaks have turned into a "work or study hour;" during which you are working to make progress toward your goal.

Although you have included others to work or collaborate with, it's also good to consider a personal coach or mentor. A personal coach can help create a plan that's specific to you. They motivate you by holding you accountable for achieving your goals. They help you come up with new ideas and strategies to accomplish your goals. You must be sure to find the right coach. Family members and friends usually don't make good coaches. The main reason is that they will not push you as hard. They don't want you to feel as if they are pressuring you. The gentleness can cause you to fail at achieving your goal. You need someone who will be like a personal "drill sergeant" to push you to the FINISH LINE!

You must be able to set yourself apart, and stand out from the crowd. Move away from the ordinary and ask yourself, "Who else has accomplished what I would like to accomplish?" Start researching, and learning what some of the successful people did to get there. It's always good to learn from the individuals who already have what you want. Where you start at is not nearly as important as where you end up.

Learn to disable your distractions. Avoid procrastination and laziness. They are some of the most common reasons for failure. So many people have worked hard at building a charisma that's out of this world. Suddenly, they fall into these traps and lose the attraction of people. Don't be one of those people. Keep the opportunities coming and keep moving in a positive manner.

Keep pushing, keep driving, and never give up. Dedicate yourself to being a champion. The great boxer, Muhammad Ali says, "Champions aren't made in gyms. Champions are made from something they have deep inside of them-a desire, a dream, a vision. They have to have the skill, and the will, but the will must be stronger than the skill." That's from the mouth of a true champion.

There is no one who can control your success. You are the only person who controls it. Don't allow anything to stand in between you and your dream. Turn a deaf ear to the naysayers and the dream stealers. Stay fired up, and keep pressing forward. Keep working smart, while focusing on your journey. While doing so, watch your life begin to turn from "tragic to magic." Once you have accomplished and fulfilled one dream, keep going. You have now proved that there are "NO BARRIERS, NO LIMITS" to living the life of your dreams!

Quotes To Help You Live Life Without Limits:

"If you don't design your own life plan, chances are you'll fall into someone else's plan. And guess what they have planned for you? Not much"......Jim Rohn

"You cannot change your destination overnight, but you can change your direction overnight"....Jim Rohn

"Life is 10% of what happens to me and 90% of how I react to it"....John Maxwell

"The greatest mistake we make is living in constant fear that we will make one."....John Maxwell

"Failure is a detour, not a dead-end street."....Zig Ziglar

"80% of success is just showing up".... Woody Allen

"You can have everything in life you want, if you will just help other people get what they want"...Zig Ziglar

"Winning isn't everything, but the will to win is everything."….Vince Lombardi

"Things turn out best for people who make the best out of the way things turn out"….John Wooden

"The best way to predict the future is to create it!"….Jason Kaufman

"There are two kinds of people in the world: those who make excuses and those who get results. An excuse person will find any excuse for why a job was not done, and a results person will find any reason why it can be done. Be a creator, not a reactor"….Alan Cohen

"Don't wish it were easier, wish you were better."….Jim Rohn

"Formal education will make you a living; self-education will make you a fortune."….Jim Rohn

"If you are not willing to risk the unusual, you will have to settle for the ordinary."….Jim Rohn

"Live life to the fullest." …. Ernest Hemingway

"Reach for the sky, set goals, live life to the fullest and always remember to wake up each day with a smile." ....Brandy Miller

"He who does not live life to it's fullest can never know the true meaning of life ..." Unknown

"To discover life to the fullest, one must start within."....Sasha Azevedo

"The key to success, and to happiness, is being fully engaged in life - leading yourself with inspiration and committed action -setting your own fine and honorable example."....Jonathan Lockwood Huie

"Life isn't about finding yourself. Life is about creating yourself."....George Bernard Shaw

"Self-care is critical to having a strong inner foundation. Taking good care of YOU means the people in your life will receive the best of you rather than what is left of you.".... Lorraine Cohen

"Only a life lived for others is a life worthwhile."….Albert Einstein

"Not life, but good life, is to be chiefly valued."…. Socrates

"Life is not about how fast you run or how high you climb but how well you bounce."….Vivian Komori

"You don't have the power to make life 'fair,' but you do have the power to make life joyful."….Jonathan Lockwood Huie

"Be an Observer of Life. Gaining wisdom from carefully observing life is not a substitute for action it is a prerequisite for informed action."….Jonathan Lockwood Huie

"So long as you have courage and a sense of humor, it is never too late to start life afresh."….Freeman Dyson

"Be happy for this moment. This moment is your life."….Anonymous

"A happy life consists not in the absence, but in the mastery of hardships."….Helen Keller

"Don't go through life - grow through life."….Eric Butterworth

"Only when life is difficult, are we challenged to become our greatest selves."….Jonathan Lockwood Huie

"Life's most urgent question is: what are you doing for others? "….Martin Luther King, Jr.

"Laugh when you can apologize when you should, and let go of what you can't change. Life's too short to be anything… but happy."….Anonymous

"Life is not about perfection - or a quest for perfection. Life is about enjoying what we have -for as long as we have it." ….Jonathan Lockwood Huie

"Don't live your life to please other people."….Oprah Winfrey

"Life is as easy or as hard as you think it is."….Jonathan Lockwood Huie

"Life isn't about waiting for the storm to pass…It's about learning to Dance in the Rain."….Vivian Greene

About the Author

Andrea Freeman was born in Baltimore, Maryland into a family of 5 children. She is the oldest of the 5 kids, and was raised in Aberdeen, Maryland for all of her childhood years. She graduated from Aberdeen High School in 1990. She took general classes at Harford Community College and later completed courses toward a Bachelor's of Science in Business Management with the University of Phoenix. In 2006, Andrea obtained her Producer License. In her spare time, Andrea enjoys reading and writing.

Andrea has had the privilege of traveling throughout Maryland, DC, Virginia, New York, Philadelphia, and other areas to speak with businesses and individuals about banking, insurance, being an entrepreneur, and the benefits of having a business.

Andrea has also taken advantage of many opportunities to speak with teenage mothers, single mothers, and women in crisis. She has been able to relate, connect, and share her personal testimony of facing some of the same challenges; and how she has been able to overcome them, while balancing everyday life, motherhood, work, and business. Andrea has been considered a great role model, a people's person, and an inspiration to many.

Andrea has 4 daughters. Shalise 26, Shanise 25, Alexus 19, and Ayana 16.

Andrea has worked at leading, building businesses, and serving others for over 20 years. She has successfully built a jewelry business called "Classy Accessories", which she started in 2008. Classy Accessories (www.classyaccessories.net) sells great quality, costume jewelry, handbags, and cosmetics at very affordable prices.

Andrea has also worked to establish a non-profit organization called **C**hanging **L**ives **A**nd **S**incerely **S**upporting **Y**ou (**C.L.A.S.S.Y.**), Inc. The mission of the organization is: To effectively increase the academic achievements, self-esteem, and life opportunities of women, through educating, inspiring, encouraging, and supporting them. The vision is: To equip and empower women throughout the world with information that would help them to re-establish their values and totally transform their lives. **C.L.A.S.S.Y.** (www.classy5.org) provides free monthly seminars, volunteers at nursing homes, supports recovering addicts, homeless shelters, the needy, sick and shut-ins, and grants college scholarships to students.

Andrea uses her writing as a tool for Christian ministry to help others deepen their love and relationship with God, and to equip them to better serve Him in all that they do. She has a passion for showing the love of Christ to those in need and believes that all believers should help by being a reflection of the character of our Lord and Savior Jesus Christ.

If you would like to write in reference to this book, request more copies or contact the author, please feel free to do so at:

Andrea Freeman
P.O. Box 18151
Baltimore, MD 21220
info@authorandreafreeman.com
www.authorandreafreeman.com
443-478-8500

www.ingramcontent.com/pod-product-compliance
Lightning Source LLC
LaVergne TN
LVHW021407080426
835508LV00020B/2483